THE *NEW* DOGSTEPS

A better understanding of dog gait
through cineradiography ("moving X-rays")

Best wishes

Rachel Page Elliott

CINERADIOGRAPHY — What it is.

At Harvard University's Museum of Comparative Zoology, a specially-equipped laboratory makes possible the simultaneous photographing and fluoroscoping of dogs as they move at controlled speeds on a treadmill. This procedure, known as cineradiography, is similar to "moving X-rays". To make the films more graphic for the layman, Mrs. Elliott has traced them in simple drawings that enable us to clearly see what happens "inside" at the corresponding stage of the dog's movement.

The *NEW* DOGSTEPS

*A better understanding of dog gait
through cineradiography ("moving X-rays")*

by RACHEL PAGE ELLIOTT

Illustrations by Eve Andrade and the author

SECOND EDITION
Third Printing—1985

HOWELL BOOK HOUSE Inc.
230 Park Avenue, New York, N. Y. 10169

Library of Congress Cataloging in Publication Data

Elliott, Rachel Page.
    The new dogsteps.

    Rev. ed. of: Dogsteps. 1973.
    Bibliography: p. 127
    1. Dogs—Anatomy. 2. Gait in animals. 3. Dogs—
Breeding. I. Title.
SF767.D6E38   1983   636.7′089276   82-23427
ISBN 0-87605-521-8

Printed in U.S.A.

To my husband,
whose patience made it possible.

RACHEL PAGE ELLIOTT has long been one of America's most respected authorities on dog gait. Her unique illustrated lectures on the subject have been hailed by audiences all over the world—throughout the United States (including Hawaii and Alaska), Canada, Mexico, England, Scotland, Wales, the Scandinavian countries, Europe and Australia—and have done much to awaken breeders to the importance of recognizing the rights and wrongs in the way dogs move.

When DOGSTEPS (largely based upon the lectures) was published in 1973, the Dog Writers Association of America acclaimed it "Best Dog Book of the Year" and it continues to be the eminent book on dog gait.

But for one with Mrs. Elliott's dedication, the pursuit of knowledge is never ending. Her continuing studies with cineradiography equipment at Harvard University's Museum of Comparative Zoology have provided fresh insights on bone and joint motion, which she presents in this important new edition.

"Pagey" Elliott was born in Lexington, Massachusetts, the youngest of a large family who shared their lives with horses, dogs and other animals. She is a graduate of Radcliffe College. With her husband Mark, a retired orthodontist, she lives on a 60-acre farm along the Concord River in Carlisle (Mass.), where they have raised three children and have enjoyed an active participation in outdoor sports.

Over the years the Elliotts have owned many breeds, but main attention has been on Golden Retrievers. Foundation of their Featherquest Kennels was Goldwood Toby, trained and handled by "Pagey", and the first Golden to earn a Utility degree in Obedience. Toby's son, Tennessee's Jack Daniels, also owner-handled, was the first New England retriever to win a qualifying stake in licensed retriever trials. The Featherquest honor roll also includes many show champions.

Mrs. Elliott currently serves on the Board of Directors of the Orthopedic Foundation for Animals. She has been active in many local and national dog clubs, and is a past president of the Golden Retriever Club of America and of the Ladies Dog Club (Mass.).

Contents

Foreword

THERE has long been need for understandable information on various points of great concern to dog breeders.

Too often, people supervise breeding of dogs without knowledge of what they are doing to the breed from an hereditary standpoint. Of the many faults that can be produced, probably the most obvious are those which contribute to lameness or poor gait.

Mrs. Elliott has recognized this need for education of dog breeders in the basics of sound gait and performance. Based upon her years of association with show and field trial dogs, study of reel after reel of movie film, and the application of her findings to her own dogs, she has prepared this fine book.

It is especially aimed for the layman, with clear simple wording and easy-to-understand drawings. Study of this material will aid all in recognizing what is good and what is faulty action, and the application of what is learned should produce rewarding results for the conscientious dog breeder.

I compliment Mrs. Elliott for her deep insight into problems, her tireless work, and her devotion to improvement of dog breeds by careful selection of parents. I hope this high quality book will be the first of a series clearly showing what can be achieved by proper breeding of dogs.

—E. W. TUCKER, D. V. M.

(Dr. Tucker is a past president of the American Veterinary Medical Association,
and of the Massachusetts Veterinary Association.)

A strong, even gait is desirable in all breeds . . .

no matter the size . . .   *the shape . . .*   *or purpose.*

Author's Introduction

THE NEW DOGSTEPS is designed to make easier the recognition of normal and faulty ways in which the dog moves.

Gait tells much about a dog's structure that is not revealed when he is standing still, for it reflects his physical coordination, balance of body and soundness. The correlation between gait and structure is frequently misunderstood, and—in a time when growing interest in dogs as family pets tends to lessen awareness of the need for stamina and working ability—its significance is often overlooked.

Sound movement contributes to the health and normal lifespan of all dogs. It is as desirable a feature in the family pet as it is important to the usefulness of dogs bred for hunting, farm work, police duty or racing; and without it, show winners can never achieve true excellence. Also, sound dogs are happier dogs. This emphasis is not to detract from the value of type and temperament, which are necessary for the preservation of any breed, but rather to underline the truth of the old saying, *"As a dog moves, so is he built."*

All dogs do not gait alike. Differences in size and shape influence their way of going. The flashy step of a small terrier, for example, or the brisk trot of a Welsh Corgi, is not the same as the easy, loose stride of Bloodhounds or Newfoundlands. And the spirited drive of proud-headed Setters lends contrast to the patient scent-trailing action of Basset Hounds. Through the centuries, man has developed various kinds of dogs to meet his needs and his fancies, and their individuality today is the result of long years of selective breeding.

Varied as dogs are, however, the principle by which they cover the ground is the same for all and is dictated by nature. This is the law of balance and gravity, which is constantly directed toward efficient forward motion with a minimum waste of effort— the key to good movement. When man upsets this law through inattention to sound structure, nature has to compensate for his mistakes with counter-balances which show up in faulty gaiting patterns.

Incorrect movement, either temporary or permanent, can also occur as a result of lameness due to sprains, breaks, cuts, bruises or other reasons, but these should be recognized for what they are and not confused with inherited defects. Faults vary in severity and frequency from dog to dog, and from breed to breed, but they are universal to the canine world—constantly challenging our search for perfection.

While one does not have to be a student of anatomy to appreciate dogs, the ability to recognize good and poor movement is basic for a working knowledge. To be sure, movement is quicker than the eye, but the educated eye knows better what to look for, and the eye that understands is not easily deceived. In the course of my study on this subject, I have taken slow-motion movies, from which I have drawn animated sequences showing various phases of leg action at different angles to the viewer. Included, also, are a few skeletal suggestions to help the reader visualize bone and joint movement beneath coat and muscles. Some of the illustrations may appear to be exaggerated—actually, they are not.

The models for discussion were selected at random solely for analysis and study, and there is no intention to associate any of the technical sketches with a particular breed—for all are vulnerable. Except for some of the pencil drawings showing dogs at work, most of the studies portray dogs moving at the trot, as this gait is generally considered best for evaluating movement as it relates to build. However, some examples of other gaits have also been included for identification and comparison.

For newcomers, interest in THE NEW DOGSTEPS may be simply in owning a good dog. Nevertheless, we hope there is something of value here for *all* dog fanciers, and particularly the many breeders who are striving to raise better puppies.

Addendum

Life is a constant process of learning, which brings deeper understanding. Since the initial publication of this book in 1973, I have been privileged to study canine bone and joint motion at Harvard University's Museum of Comparative Zoology, where there is a specially equipped laboratory for simultaneously photographing and fluoroscoping animals as they move at controlled speeds on a treadmill. The procedure is known as cineradiography, similar to "moving X-rays".

My investigation was at first oriented toward the study of hip dysplasia. Not surprisingly, this led to other aspects of dog structure and answered numerous questions that have long puzzled me, particularly in regard to the dog's front assembly, how it really functions, and why a 45-degree slope of the shoulder blade is only a myth—in contradiction to the many writings that describe such an angle as essential to ideal conformation. The findings were further substantiated by lateral view X-rays of dogs in standing position. What we have failed to recognize is the great mobility of the shoulder blade as it lifts and swings in coordination with the upper arm, and the crucial influence of shape of the ribcage and muscular forces on both. The cineradiography also shows beyond doubt why a normally built dog tends to single track rather than move with its legs parallel.

It is with a feeling of responsibility that I share the radiographic findings with fellow dog fanciers, for I realize how ideas that upset or challenge long-standing theories or concepts can create controversy. I do not aim to persuade—I offer the new material in this edition only to present and discuss the findings as they have been revealed to me.

—RACHEL PAGE ELLIOT
1983

Acknowledgments

MUCH APPRECIATION is extended to the many friends who have helped, directly or indirectly, in the compilation of this material, and whose interest and enthusiasm have contributed to bringing *The New Dogsteps* to completion. This new edition has involved their continued cooperation, not only in time but also in making dogs available for the fluoroscopic study of bone and joint motion—a study that opens our eyes to the reality of the working skeleton.

I am grateful to the staff at Harvard University's Museum of Comparative Zoology where I was allowed access to special laboratory facilities, and especially to Dr. Farish Jenkins, Professor of Biology and Curator of Vertebrate Paleontology at the Museum. Dr. Jenkins' help, together with a generous grant from the Orthopedic Foundation for Animals, made this study possible. Dr. Peter Morey of the Carlisle Animal Hospital, also contributed to the study through his cooperation in taking X-rays of dogs in standing position.

My sister, Priscilla Rose, gave many valuable suggestions for the text of this book, not the least of which is the title, and two artists, Margaret Estey and our son-in-law, Maris Platais, have given wise counsel about my diagrammatic illustrations. Thanks, too, to Eve Andrade whose pencil drawings of dogs at work bring life to the text. A silent partner through all of this study has been Dr. Edgar Tucker of the Concord Animal Hospital. Dr. Tucker's dedication to the education of the dog laity in the interest of sound structure and stable temperament has been a constant source of inspiration.

Finally, I join many other writers in giving recognition to my publisher, Elsworth Howell, on whom we can always depend for encouragement and constructive guidance.

1.

The Language of Dog Anatomy
and
Comparative Skeletons

Terms Commonly Used in Describing the Dog's Outer Appearance

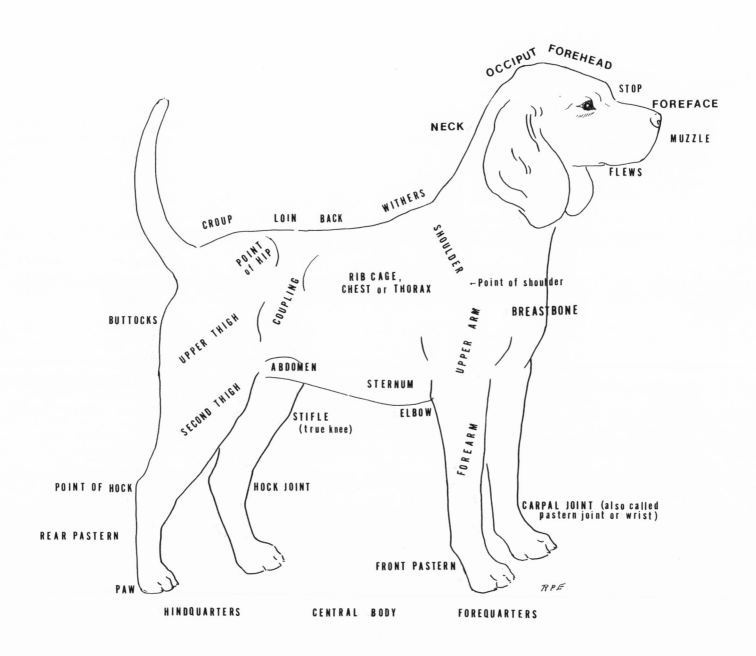

Terms Must Be Understood To Be Meaningful

To MAKE CERTAIN that we are all speaking the same language in the pages that follow, skeletal diagrams of the dog, the horse and man are included here. All three of these species share the same scientific nomenclature, but much of the common language used around dogs comes from the paddock. A few words have become misconstrued or ambiguous due to the present gap between dog and horse followers, or through translation from other languages, but most of the parlance remains intact.

In spite of their structural differences—and there are important ones—horses and dogs share much in common, and the principles applying to sound conformation and gait are applicable to both. Both vary in breed type according to purpose, both come in various shapes and sizes, and both exhibit gaiting characteristics that are influenced by the differences. Describing the horse and the dog are such expressions as *body balance*, *smooth* or *choppy action, steep* or *sloping shoulders, long* or *short coupled, well ribbed up, straight of hock* or *stifle, cowhocks, twisting* or *sickle hocks, weak* or *strong pasterns, flipping, pounding, paddling, winging, overreaching,* etc. With what other animal is the dog compared so compatably?

Even so, there are some dog fanciers who talk of their dogs in terms applicable to man—perhaps because of the lack of opportunity for first hand acquaintance with horses. For example, the carpal joint is referred to as the wrist, the stifle joint as the knee, or the hock as the heel; and because the dog is actually a toe-walker, the entire area from hock to paw is spoken of as the foot. The word "hock" is one of the more seriously misconstrued words in the canine language because it is often confused with the rear pastern. Breed standards, in describing conformation, usually call for good or moderate bend of hock. This is a justified qualification, but the unwary newcomer can be easily misled if someone tells him his dog should stand "straight in the hock" (for show purposes), when the reference is actually to the rear pastern.

The double meaning and interchange of terms can be perplexing, but fortunately the confusion is something we get accustomed to as we gain understanding and confidence. Perhaps of more serious concern are the misleading and conflicting references relating to the way dogs should or should not move. Mindful of this, readers are urged to look into the works on anatomy and locomotion listed on Page 127. In spite of their differing opinions, they are a worthwhile addition to a dog owner's library.

Comparative Skeletal Diagrams

ILIUM   LUMBAR VERTEBRAE (7)   THORACIC VERTEBRAE (13)
withers (1st 9 dorsal spines)

PELVIS

ISCHIUM

FEMUR

hip joint

SCAPULA

scapula spine

CERVICAL VERTEBRAE (7)

MANUBRIUM
breastbone

HUMERUS
upper arm

PATELLA
STIFLE JOINT

TARSALS
hock

STERNEBRAE

TIBIA

FIBULA

ULNA   RADIUS

METATARSALS
rear pastern

METACARPALS
front pastern

CARPAL JOINT

PHALANGES PEDIS
toes

PHALANGES MANIS
toes

RPE

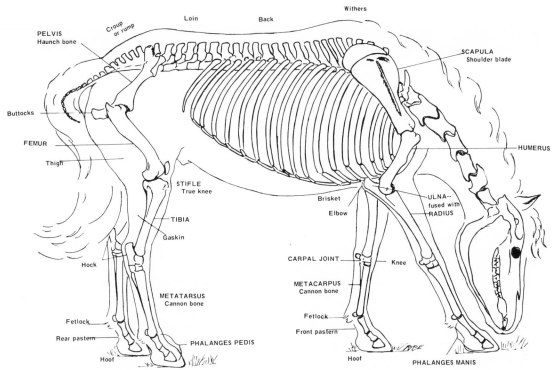

PELVIS
Haunch bone

Croup or rump

Loin   Back   Withers

SCAPULA
Shoulder blade

Buttocks

FEMUR

Thigh

STIFLE
True knee

Brisket

Elbow

ULNA--
fused with
RADIUS

HUMERUS

TIBIA

Gaskin

CARPAL JOINT   Knee

Hock

METACARPUS
Cannon bone

METATARSUS
Cannon bone

Fetlock

Rear pastern

PHALANGES PEDIS

Fetlock

Front pastern

Hoof

PHALANGES MANIS

Hoof

Evolution has changed the horse into a weight-carrying animal, chiefly by altering his legs from the hock and the knee down. He used to walk on four toes in front and three in back, but now walks on a single toe in each foot. Though there is but a semblance of some of the original bones left in his legs, the scientific names remain, and horses and dogs still share the same principles of locomotion. Notice the horse's greater number of ribs, in contrast to the dog.

PELVIS
Hip bone   SACRUM

COCCYX

SCAPULA

Hip joint

Shoulder joint

FEMUR
Thigh bone

HUMERUS
Upper arm

Elbow

FIBULA

Forearm

TIBIA
Shin bone

ULNA

RADIUS

PATELLA
Knee joint

Heel

CARPAL JOINT
Wrist

TARSALS
Ankle joint

METATARSALS

METACARPALS

PHALANGES PEDIS
Toes

PHALANGES MANIS
Fingers

19

Code to the gait diagrams in this book:

Front paw—   *Rear paw—*

Sample:

The Pace

Paws connected with dotted line move as a pair.

2.

Gait Patterns Defined

The Natural Gaits—

THE term **gait** means pattern of footsteps at various rates of speed, each pattern distinguished by a particular rhythm and footfall. The *walk,* the *trot,* and the *gallop* are perhaps the most commonly recognized of the gaits, but *ambling, pacing,* and *cantering* are also normal ways in which many four-footed animals move.

The two gaits acceptable in the show ring are the walk and the trot. When a judge requests an exhibitor to "Gait your dog," he means simply that the dog be led (usually at the trot) across the ring and back, so that he may evaluate the dog's way of moving and how it relates to his conformation.

THE WALK seems so uncomplicated there is no need to analyze it other than to draw contrast with the faster gaits which cause the dog to rely on speed for balance and stability. At the walk, three legs are in support of the body at all times, each foot lifting from the ground one at a time in regular sequence. The pattern of footfall is right hind, right front, left hind, left front.

THE AMBLE is like a fast rocking walk with an *irregular four-beat cadence* in which the legs on either side move *almost*—but not quite—as a pair. This relaxed, easy movement is characteristic of a few large breeds, but all dogs amble now and then. Often seen as a transition movement between the walk and faster gaits, ambling should not be confused with pacing.

THE PACE is *a two-beat lateral gait,* in which the legs on each side move back and forth exactly as a pair, causing a rolling or rocking motion of the dog's body. Structure and proportion have a direct influence on a dog's inclination to pace. This gait is characteristic of a few large breeds, but it is frowned upon in the show ring. The action is sometimes called "side-wheeling."

Early pacing horses, at first not fully appreciated for their racing potential, were dubbed "side-wheelers", a term from steamboat terminology. The long legs and great speed of modern pacers minimizes body roll.

THE TROT is a rhythmic two-beat diagonal gait in which the feet at diagonally opposite ends of the body strike the ground together, i.e. right hind with left front and left hind with right front. Because only two feet are on the ground at a time, the dog must rely on forward momentum for balance.

At a normal trot, when the weight is transferred from one pair of legs to the other, there is a slight, almost imperceptible, period of suspension as the body is propelled forward. Some people call this "spring." In a dog of the above proportions, the imprint of the hind feet tend to cover the tracks left by the front.

Diagonal leg action distinguishes trotters from pacers among harness horses.

HACKNEY GAITING is a variation of the trot, distinguished by *high flashy action* in the front and rear legs. To be correct, the topline should remain as level as possible as the dog moves, all the action being in the exaggerated flexing of the joints. This gait is characteristic of a few small breeds.

The term derives from hackney horses which are bred specifically for this type of action.

THE SUSPENSION, or **FLYING TROT,** is a fast gait in which forward thrust contributes to a longer and more plainly discernible period of flight during each half stride. Because of the long "reach", the oncoming hind feet step beyond the imprint left by the front. Coordination and good foot timing are of great importance to avoid interference.

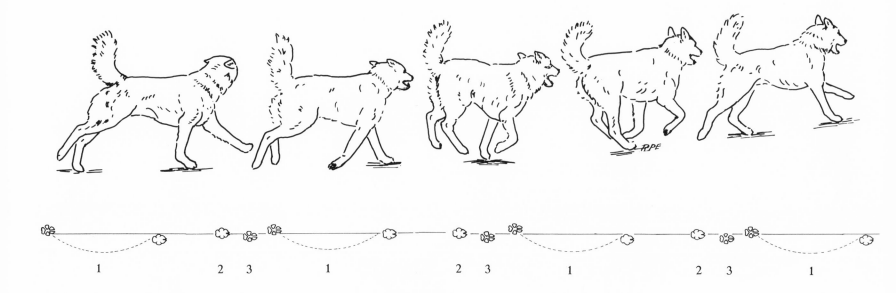

| | 1 | | 2 | 3 | 1 | | 2 | 3 | 1 | | 2 | 3 | 1 |

THE CANTER, a gait slower than the gallop and not as tiring, *has three beats to each stride*—two legs moving separately and two as a diagonal pair. When the dog "leads" with the left front foot (as in this illustration), the right front moves simultaneously with the left rear. Cantering is sometimes referred to as the "collected gallop" or the "lope", but such references are to rate of speed rather than pattern of footfall, as they differ from the canter in this last respect.

Sound sled dogs cover the miles at a steady "lope".

THE GALLOP, fastest of the gaits, has a *four-beat rhythm,* and often an extra period of suspension during which the body is propelled through the air with all four feet off the ground. I have seen no better description of the gallop than the following, written by the famous canine authority, "Stonehenge":*

> Perfection of the gallop depends upon the power of extending the shoulders and forelegs as far as possible, as well as bringing the hind legs rapidly forward to give the propulsive stroke. If the hindquarters are good and well-brought into action, while the shoulders do not thrust the forelegs well forward, the action is laboured and slow. On the contrary, if the shoulders do their duty, but the hind legs are not brought well forward, or do not thrust the body onwards with sufficient force, the action may be elegant, but it is not powerful and rapid. For these purposes, therefore, we require good shoulders, good thighs, a good back, and good legs, and, lastly, for lodging the lungs and heart, whose actions are essential for the maintenance of speed, a well-formed and capacious chest.

———————

* "Stonehenge": *The Dogs of the British Islands,* Second Edition, London 1872, p. 180.

A combination of sound conformation, good balance, and the spirit to win, pay off as galloping race hounds near the finish line.

3.

Good Performance
Is the Test of
Good Structure

Dogs that are built well can stand long days of hard work.

A good working dog has limbs that extend freely . . .
and balance of body for trotting long hours without tiring.

This type of farm dog will drive a herd of cows and should be able to dodge kicking heels because of its low frame.

Good proportion and strong loins lend suppleness to the back...

Strong pasterns and thick pads help reduce the shock of sudden impact.

36

Strong hindquarters provide strength for quick bursts of speed . . .

. . . and thrust for leaping.

Function influences form. For example, here is a variety of dog developed through selective breeding to ferret out farm pests from underground. The elbows became set above the line of the brisket in order to free the legs for digging, while the dog's weight came to rest on his chest. The long and gradual upward slant of the lower rib cage helps him to slide more easily over rocks and roots—a handy arrangement in case there is need for speedy retreat.

4.

Angulation and Balance

Foundation of Structure and Movement

The Importance of Angulation

ESSENTIAL to the appearance and qualities of endurance in all dogs are the structural features that govern balance and the ability to move freely—called "angulation." Good angulation means effortless stride and smooth action. Poor angulation tends to shorten stride, cause irregularities in gaiting patterns or make a dog's movement stilted and choppy.

Angulation has to do with the slant of the bones and size of the angles at certain joints. Those influencing structure and gait most are the shoulder and hip joints, formed by the largest, strongest bones in the dog's body. These joints counterbalance one another as they lift, open and shut with the swing of the limbs. The front of the dog normally carries about 60% of the total body weight and works like a shock-absorbing mechanism as it coordinates with drive from the hindquarters and absorbs impact with the ground. Whether viewed from the side or from front or rear, the action should be smooth and harmonious with no jerking or twisting. Problems result when one part of the body has to overwork or compensate for lack of balance, injury or weakness in another.

There are generally ideal measurements for every form or figure, and authorities on canine anatomy have been no exception in drawing up standards of physical perfection for the many kinds of dogs in the world today. In each standard the outward appearance of the breed is described, with angulation specified or inferred because of its importance to overall conformation. Variations occur depending on the jobs dogs are expected to perform, and in differences within individual members of the same breed—correct or faulty. Width and depth of chest, for example, affect the relationship of the shoulder blade and the upper arm, and the angle at which they join. Length and set of the upper arm determines the position of the elbow against the chest wall. Normally, the humerus should counterbalance the angle of the shoulder blade. Elbows that set too far back or too far forward can throw the front assembly out of balance and adversely affect the dog's way of moving.

Rear angulation can be influenced by the length and set of the pelvic assembly in relation to the spinal column (to which it is connected at the sacrum) and by the relative length of the leg bones. Hip joints consist of ball and socket construction with considerable rotating facility, while action of the stifles and hocks is hinge-like. These joints all share a vital role in providing strength and drive to locomotion.

Excessive angulation in any part of the dog's body is detrimental to joint support and endurance. It is never a question of the more angulation the better—it is a matter of just how much is needed for functional efficiency.

GOOD ANGULATION facilitates a smooth, ground-covering stride. Balance facilitates good foot-timing. Joints that control movement should flex easily and smoothly, providing strong thrust from the rear with spring and resilience in the forehand. The swing and extension of the forelegs should coordinate with action of the rear so that there will be no over-stepping or interfering. As a general rule, the feet should move rather close to the ground so as to avoid excessive bending of the joints, which can be inefficient and tiring.

POOR ANGULATION shortens stride because the bones meeting at the shoulder joints and hips are steeply set, forming joints with wide open angles. Swing of the blades and the upper arms is restricted, as is bend and thrust from the rear. Dogs so constructed must take shorter steps, and more of them, to get where they are going, and their action is bouncing rather than smooth. This dog is too straight, both front and rear, but in spite of this fault and a short stilted gait, his body appears to be in balance and he may be better off than a dog lacking balance, where one end has to compensate for faultiness in the other.

"Practically the whole propelling force of the hind limb is dependent on the ability of the dog to straighten the leg from the state of angulation to complete extension, as forcibly and as rapidly as may be required. This is dependent entirely upon the muscle power of a well-developed second thigh."

—Smythe: *Conformation of the Dog.*

"Sickle hocks" (*fault*)

Contrasting sharply with the suppleness of the dog on the previous page is this dog with "sickle hocks." The term is derived from the sickle, a farm tool with a rigid angle where the handle meets the blade. Sickle-hocked action is stiff and shuffling, with almost no use of the hock joint to help in forward propulsion. A sickle-hocked dog usually stands with his pasterns angled slightly forward, never standing "well up on his hocks." In this particular dog, the front quarters are very straight, and because of almost no push from the rear, most of his energy is spent bobbing up and down.

The Value of Balance

BALANCE depends not only on the proportion of head to neck, depth of chest to length of legs, and overall length of body to height, but also on a front end that matches the rear. In other words, when a dog is standing naturally, the angulation at the shoulder and hip joints should be approximately equal, in order to provide the same amount of reach in the forelegs as in the rear.

A dog is not in balance if the shoulder and upper arm are steeply set and the hindquarters are well-angulated, because he will have a short stride in front and a long stride in the rear. Conversely, he is not in balance if the front is well-angulated but the hindquarters are steep, because this will mean good reach in front but a shorter stride in the rear—and the front quarters will overwork. It is possible for a dog that is equally steep fore and aft to be in balance—and he may be better off than one that lacks balance—but he will not have the quality of movement that is achieved when balance is combined with good angulation.

Lack of structural balance is the reason for much incorrect gaiting. A few illustrations of this point may be seen on the next seven pages.

OVERREACHING at the trot is a common fault, caused by more angulation and drive from behind than in front, so that the rear feet are forced to step to one side of the forefeet to avoid interfering or clipping. This is one of the many forms of poor foot-timing, but it must not be confused with the natural overreach in the suspension trot, or in the canter or gallop.

"Overreaching," Due to More Height than Length (*fault*)

Overreaching is a common fault in puppies as they develop through "leggy" stages when height at the withers may exceed length from buttocks to shoulder joint by a fractional difference. Interesting action is illustrated here in that this young dog places his right hind foot first to the outside of the front leg, and then to the inside in the effort to avoid striking. He is also "padding", which means that the forelimbs lift too high, throwing the striking phase of the paws out of rhythm with expended thrust from the rear. In other words, the right forelimb should strike the ground just as the rear paw on the same side has pushed off. The diagonals as well are uncoordinated. The diagonal legs should work almost in unison.

HACKNEY ACTION *as a fault* is caused by more angulation and drive from behind than in front, but instead of overreaching the dog resorts to a quick, extra high action of the forelegs in order to keep the paws out of the way of the oncoming back feet. The action is bouncy rather than smooth, as evidenced by the tips of this little dog's ears, which flip up and down with each step. Cute as it may appear to ringside spectators, hackneying is a waste of energy and very tiring. It should not be confused with the normal hackney action characteristic of a few small breeds whose high action is confined to leg joints and achieved only through proper angulation.

"Padding" and "Running Downhill" (*faults*)

"PADDING" is a compensating action to offset constant concussion when a straight front is subjected to overdrive, or too much thrust, from the rear. The front feet flip upward in a split-second delaying action to better coordinate stride of the forelimbs with the longer stride from behind. This tends to keep the front feet from slamming into the ground and thus helps to lessen the pounding through steeply-set pasterns and shoulder bones. The action is almost too quick for the eye to follow, as the front feet land carefully, far back on the heels, with the thickest part of the pads acting as buffers against impact with the ground. Strain on the front quarters is accentuated when a dog is lower at the withers than in the hindquarters, as illustrated here. Such structure gives him the appearance of **"running downhill**."

Faulty Topline—"Running Downhill"

Youth has its problems. Puppies often develop faster in the rear end than in the front, which gives them the appearance of running downhill even though they are on level ground. Long dogs with short legs never have to cope with the inconvenience of rear feet overstepping the front, but lack of balance still impairs symmetry and overall appearance.

Good level topline.

"POUNDING" is another gaiting fault which results from the dog's stride being shorter in front than in the rear. The forefeet strike the ground before the rear stride is expended. If a dog with this fault does nothing to spare himself, such as "padding", "hackneying" or pacing, the thrust from the hindquarters causes the front feet to hit the ground hard, as happens when a person is pushed suddenly and is forced to take a quick step before his joints can properly "give" to cushion the impact. In the dog, such impact has a pile-driving effect through pasterns and shoulder bones, causing abrupt choppy action at the withers. Constant "pounding" tends to bruise joint cartilage, and may eventually cause the dog to "break down in front."

Good Front Pasterns

STRONG PASTERNS almost invariably keep company with good fronts because they are part of the bone assembly that receives and cushions impact with the ground. Good pasterns and strong carpal joints have kinetic spring and resilience.

"Knuckling Over" (*fault*)

"Knuckling over" in the carpal joint is sometimes referred to as "over at the knees." Technically, this is known as hyperextension of the carpal joint. It is a serious fault that throws the front quarters out of balance. The expression "knuckling over" is also used in reference to hyperextension of the hock.

"Broken Pasterns" and "Overreaching" (*faults*)

A straight front with low withers forces this dog to land heavily with each step. Constant pounding has weakened ligaments and tendons in the pasterns to the point where they bend far too much as the dog's weight passes over the front quarters. Also called "down at the pasterns."

How Angulation Affects
Muscle Structure

Iₙ the preceding pages, angulation has been discussed as it relates to length of stride and to balance. Another important consideration is how it affects muscle structure.

Dog "A" illustrates how good angulation gives wider spread to the muscles, due to the fact that the shoulder bones and the pelvis are properly slanted. This slant seems to provide more area for muscle attachment and lends strength and substance to the dog's appearance. Good angulation also goes hand-in-hand with a strong middle piece, and with a rib cage that extends well back.

Correct placement of the scapula, called "good shoulder layback", contributes to Dog "A's" reach of neck and good head carriage, and gives the neckline a pleasing transition into the withers and topline. In conformation terms, this is referred to as a "neck well-set-on" or "setting well into the shoulders."

Dog "B's" upright structure in both front and rear quarters illustrates how poor angulation tends to reduce the size and slant of the bones and affects the area of muscle attachment. In this type of dog, these bones are usually narrower, with the muscles relatively poorly developed, and it may be said the dog "lacks substance." In addition, steep shoulders detract from the dog's overall appearance because the neckline joins the withers abruptly and tends to make the neck look short.

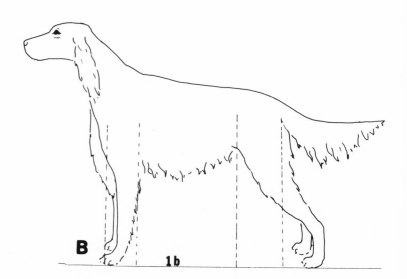

Dotted lines in these two studies call attention to differences in width across front and rear quarters, and show at a glance that the dog with greater width has better angulation. Correct positioning of the shoulder and pelvis always lends breadth to the quarters (viewed in profile), from shoulder joint to a line dropped just behind the blade, and from the forward edge of the pelvis to the buttocks. It is such structure that clues us in to the better movers, whatever the breed of dog, for the principles and advantages of good angulation are the same for all.

DOG "A"—Illustrating how good angulation provides the foundation for good muscle structure, lending breadth to the front and rear quarters and substance to the overall picture.

DOG "B"—illustrating how poor angulation limits the foundation for muscle structure, narrowing the width across front and rear quarters, and giving the appearance of less substance.

55

Estimating Angulation

WHEN one talks about angles and bone lengths in a live dog, it is important to realize that there can be no exact determination. Figures are only approximate and judgments vary depending on who does the measuring, how it is done, and which bone prominences are used as landmarks. Muscles are never stable and appearances may change through handling, training, and general condition. Even as a dog stands naturally, the slightest shift in posture or turn of the head can alter the picture. However, in spite of such uncertainties, dog fanciers will no doubt always attempt to assess angulation by means of measuring tools. A goniometer is a handy implement for this purpose. Such efforts will at least serve to train the eye in what to look for, or the hands in what to feel for.

Front Quarters

A common method for evaluating slant and placement of the bones in the front assembly is to take a line from the uppermost edge of the scapula (**A**) to the foremost prominence of the humerus (**B**) and go from there to the elbow (**E**). As a general rule, the distance between these points of reference should look or feel about equal, and if the front is balanced the elbow will set approximately on or close to an imaginary vertical line dropped from the caudal, or posterior, angle of the blade (**C**). These are not actual bone measurements, only landmarks that can be easily palpated. It is important that the dog stand naturally with its legs perpendicular to the ground.

Another way to assess angulation is to feel the scapula ridge that runs up the near center of the blade and figure the angle of an imaginary vertical line dropped from the upper tip to the ground. The slant of the humerus may be determined by a line from its upper center (**D**) to its lowest end (**G**), not to the elbow. These measurements will differ from those taken by the method described above, but the findings are more realistic as to the actual bone placement and joint angulation.

Note that a line extended upward along the scapula ridge concurs with the apex of **T-2**, which is the second of the nine thoracic spines (*spinous processes*) that form the withers. While slight variation may occur between **T-1** and **T-3**, depending on conformation or shift in body posture, radiographic studies reveal **T-2** as the normal location for the upper tip of the scapula in the average dog.

The dotted line **A-L** shows how a slope of 45 degrees would set the scapula at such an angle as to place the shoulder joint in advance of the breastbone where the entire assembly would lack muscular support of the chest wall, and the joint itself would not have such strong bracing. (*See also page 67.*) The text explains later why from such a position the lift and inward swing of the blade would tend to interfere with the cervical structures.

Hindquarters

In the hindquarters, length of the croup and bend of stifle and hock are more clearly visible, or at least are easy to feel under a heavy coat. However, variables in measurement can occur here as well, depending on how the dog stands; he may be crouching due to uneasiness or standing roached because of discomfort. Length and slope of the pelvic assembly can be approximated by taking a line from the forward edge of the ilium (**I**) to the ischium, or buttock (**J**). However, the exact location of the point of the buttock can be misleading because its shape and tilt may differ with the type of dog.

Pelvic slope and outline of the croup are not one and the same. While the outline of the croup and set-on of tail may be influenced by slant of the pelvis, the outline seems to be more directly affected by the arch, dip or straightness of the lumbar section, together with the way the sacro-iliac bones attach to the inside of the wings of the ilium. The dog's tail is but a continuation of the spine.

56

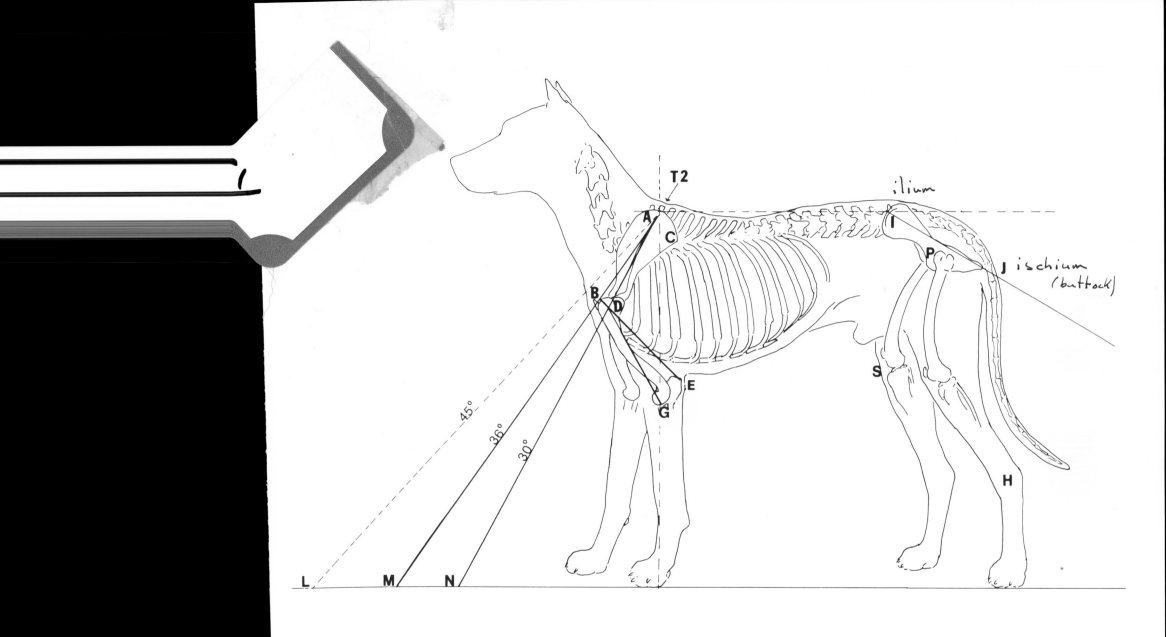

Variations in skeletal framework relate to the work dogs have been bred to do, to man's emphasis on the exotica rather than functional soundness, or to interference with working structure through injudicious breeding programs. A dog's job qualifications must be clearly understood, for the differences influence angulation and are reflected in individual gaiting styles as well as in quality of performance.

Dogs are often posed in a show stance to accentuate bend of stifle and hock, a position that drops the topline and changes the angle of the pelvic assembly. The above sketch shows what may be acceptable rear angulation for this kind of dog. However, excessive angulation, even temporary, can weaken joint support.

Two illustrations showing what is meant by a "**neck well set on**." Good necklines merge gradually with strong withers at the base of the neck and form a pleasing transition into the back. The slightest shift in leg position can alter the appearance of the front assembly.

FLAT WITHERS usually indicate upright shoulder blades which can create an abrupt juncture at the base of the neck. The blades tend to set too far forward and the neckline appears short. However, this is not always the case because some upright blades set too far back and the neckline may appear long. Longhaired dogs are sometimes groomed to disguise faulty fronts, but actual lay of the scapula can be determined by feeling for it. Horsemen who know structure avoid animals with steep shoulders and flat withers, not only because upright blades mean a hard pounding ride, but also because flat withers let the saddle slide forward.

Here is **a good neckline** above an obliquely set shoulder blade, combined with correct angulation in the rear. However, the upper arm tends to set more upright than the scapula, which positions the elbow further forward along the chest wall. Such a foreassembly is often found in "squarely built" terrier breeds, giving rise to the old horseman's expression, "Built like a cleverly made hunter—short in the back, but standing over a lot of ground." Notice length of the pelvic assembly—and particularly the ischium (buttock) in contrast to the terrier below.

Zach?

A short neckline joining flat withers above steeply-set shoulders tends to give undesirable length to the back, particularly when combined with a steeply-set rear.

5.

Understanding Fronts

—An Inside Look

Cineradiography
Casts New Light On
A Much Discussed Subject

THERE seems to be more misunderstanding about the front structure of the dog than of any other part of its anatomy, probably because the bones making up the fore assembly are not visible to the naked eye, nor clearly pictured through feel. In the Introduction to this edition of THE NEW DOGSTEPS I mentioned that my search for answers to questions that have long puzzled me led to a study of bone and joint motion at Harvard University's Museum of Comparative Zoology, where specially designed equipment makes possible the simultaneous photographing and fluoroscoping of dogs as they move on a treadmill.

The technique is known as **cineradiography.** Taken on 16mm film, the results are similar to moving X-rays which reveal the dog's remarkable skeletal machinery from the side as well as from underneath the body.

Dogs representing a variety of type and conformation were used in the study. Except at the gallop, the subjects moved on the treadmill at average trotting speed. In addition to the cineradiography, a number of still X-rays were taken of dogs in standing position, rather than lying on their side, to show the natural setting of the shoulder assembly as it bears the weight of the trunk. The radiographic findings take the guesswork out of what really goes on and challenge some long-standing notions.

Tracing from single 16mm movie frame of a Collie moving at a moderate trot. Dotted lines indicate free excursion of the shoulder assembly as the blades swing from their upper edges. At a moderate trot, the excursion is about 30 degrees.

At the gallop, the excursion is much greater.

30°

There is a human tendency to accept what appears in print as having withstood some incredible truth test. A case in point is the long held belief that a 45-degree slope of the shoulder blade is necessary for providing maximum extension or reach of the forelimb, and this is written into many breed standards. I have often wondered about the illusiveness of this ideal, for I have never found it myself, and it was not until given the opportunity to observe skeletal action through cineradiography that I realized why such a position would be a mechanical impossibility to the dog's function. A 45-degree slant, or layback, would be workable if the blade were a stationary bone with a more or less fixed joint from which the upper arm moved forward and back. But this is not the case.

What we have failed to recognize is the great mobility of the shoulder blade as partner to the action of the upper arm, which serves as a lever in lifting and transporting the central body forward as smoothly as possible.

At a moderate trot, the blade swings from its upper rim with an excursion, lift and fall, of about 30 degrees. At the gallop, the excursion is much greater. (*See drawings, facing page.*) As the assembly lifts, it also swings inward, leaving the supportive role of the chest wall. If the motion *began* from a 45-degree position, the scapula would lift too high and the "medial component of the shoulder

musculature would force the shoulder to bear directly on cervical structures." (F. A. Jenkins).

Radiographic studies show that as a dog stands with the forelegs beneath him, a blade set at about 30 degrees—measured up the scapula ridge off a vertical plane—is within normal limits for the average well-built dog. We must try to visualize the anatomical limitations within which the shoulder and upper arm are held against the ribcage, and the way in which chest shape and muscling influence the position of both. The combined factors not only influence shoulder excursion, but also explain why a dog single-tracks or moves with a wider footfall.

The humerus is a strong bone shaft, normally longer than the scapula, that slopes down and back into the elbow. Its position and relationship with the shoulder blade varies with functional type and may be correct or faulty within members of the same breed. The differences influence angulation and placement of the elbow against the chest wall and, as previously stated, are reflected in particular gaiting styles and in the quality of performance.

The following discussion in no way lessens the importance of good shoulder layback; it is directed toward a clearer understanding of what constitutes a normal front and how the assembly functions as a whole.

In the absence of a collar bone, maximum muscular support of the chest wall is needed when the dog is at rest and for control of the limbs when the dog is in motion. *Many differences occur in the way dogs are built, but in each one the ligaments, tendons and muscles originate and insert on the same anatomical parts, and accordingly establish the boundaries within which the scapula is positioned against the chest wall.* Normally the blade's lower edge joins the upper arm at the joint just back of the breastbone, and from there it slants in toward the spinous processes that form the withers. The trapezius muscles that flow forward over the lower neck and rearward over the back anchor on either side of the scapula spine, play a vital role in holding the shoulder blades in place, and in lifting and retracting the blade as the dog moves. (*See page 55, figures A-3a and B-3b.*)

INDEX

A—acromion (point of shoulder)
C—cervical (neck)
E—elbow
F—sternum
f—sternbrae
H—humerus (upper arm)
L—lumbar vertebrae
M—manubrium (breastbone)
P—pelvis
S—scapula (shoulder blade)
s—scapula spine (or ridge)
T—spinous processes of the thoracic vertebrae
(9 in all, forming the withers)

Normal Shoulder Position

Tracing from a lateral X-ray of the shoulder assembly of a dog in natural standing position, showing optimum joint and muscular support against the chest wall. This dog has a balanced front structure, with the scapula slanting at approximately 30 degrees off a vertical plane. (*Note:* The Collie that was the subject of this tracing is drawn in motion on Page 64.)

Unnatural Shoulder Position

Tracing from a lateral X-ray of a dog lying on its side, with the scapula pulled forward to simulate a 45-degree slope. The upper blade is in the area of T-2, where the trapezius and the rhomboidus muscles hold it in place, but the shoulder joint is forced into an unrealistic and non-functional position far in advance of the breastbone. Were the dog actually standing this way, the supportive role of the thoracic (chest) wall would be absent, and in action the upward and inward swing of the blade would force the musculature to bear on the neck structures.

A Few Variables

THOUGH the shoulder assembly is always in the same area of the dog's body, subtle differences in shape of the chest can affect its placing and the overall quality of movement. Ribcages vary in depth, length and breadth. Some have good arc and spring, others drop flat and straight. Some widen quickly near the forechest, others may be narrow. Variations also occur in the length and forward thrust of the individual sternebrae between the lower ribs which form the floor of the chest. Too, there may be slight diversities in height and slant of the withers, or in the vertebral lengths that separate them, however minute. All of these factors influence angulation singly or in combination.

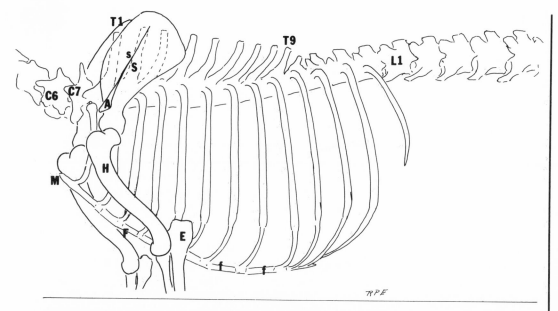

Tracing from radiograph of a Cairn Terrier taken in standing position. Layback of the shoulder is within normal range of 30 degrees and there is balanced relationship with the humerus against the chest wall. The upper rims of the scapulae are above the apex of the withers, which might indicate looseness in the front assembly as the dog moves. Because of roaching the topline is poor. Notice that the roach begins at the 10th spinal vertebra.

INDEX

A— acromion (point of shoulder)
C— cervical (neck)
E— elbow
F— sternum
f— sternbrae
H— humerus (upper arm)
L— lumbar vertebrae
M— manubrium (breastbone)
P— pelvis
S— scapula (shoulder blade)
s— scapula spine (or ridge)
T— spinous processes of the thoracic vertebrae (9 in all, forming the withers)

Tracing from radiograph of a Shih Tzu in standing position. The shoulder blade is almost vertical, pointing upward toward T-1. This assembly is out of balance, giving the appearance of the dog "setting over himself." Were this little dog stripped of its coat an abrupt juncture at the base of the neck would be clearly visible. In contrast to the diagram of the Cairn on the facing page, the upper edges of the shoulder blades set below the rise of the withers.

Tracing from radiograph of a Siberian Husky taken in standing position, showing the shoulder and upper arm set too far back along a narrow, shallow chest. While some prominence of the breastbone is desirable for the attachment of the "pulley" muscles that advance the central body and control swing of the forelimbs, too much prominence gives rise to the term "pigeon breasted."

breast
bone
manubrium

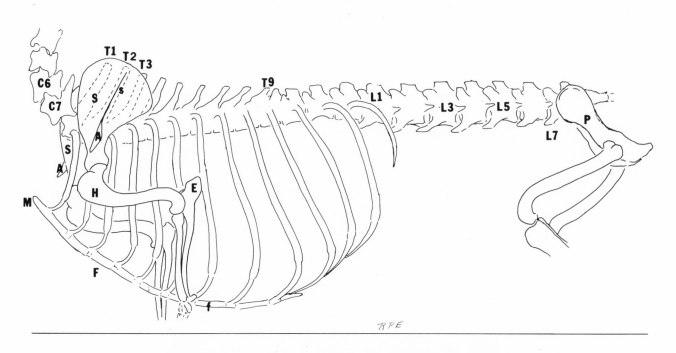

Above is a tracing from a radiograph of a Miniature Wirehaired Dachshund taken in standing position. The shoulder assembly is out of balance and the chest line is abnormally low, even for this type of dog. Notice the upward tilt of the ischium (buttock).

At left and right are sketches of the same Doxie, traced from 16mm movie frames. Because of faulty placement of the elbows, the upper arms cannot coordinate efficiently with the blades, and the legs therefore swing outward more than forward, resulting in **paddling** and **padding.**

Paddling

Padding

6.

Mobility and Excursion of
the Shoulder Assembly

The following skeletal studies of shoulder action are drawn from individual 16mm movie frames made by means of cineradiography. The diagrams show progressive phases of the front assembly functioning as a unit with slight opening and closing of the shoulder joint. Due to limited size of the camera field, it was not possible to include the entire dog.

Each stride phase is correlated as closely as possible with similar positions of the dog sketched beneath. The latter studies were drawn from regular 16mm film frames.

SHOULDER MOVEMENT AT THE TROT

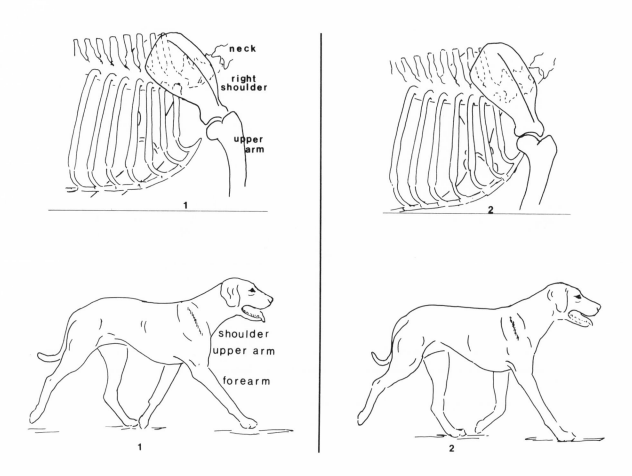

A good shoulder assembly has the flexibility to lift and fold like a shock absorbing mechanism as it absorbs impact with the ground and carries the central body smoothly foward. The upper arms serve as levers to lift the blades which simultaneously pivot from their upper edge where they lie in against the withers. When I say "pivot" I mean a slight swiveling or elliptical motion, because the amount of movement is controlled by muscles which in turn are affected by conformation of the chest and the dog's physical condition.

Shoulder Movement at the Trot (*continued*)

In forward motion the shoulder loses most of the supportive role of the chest wall and must rely on muscles for stability. There is no collar bone between its lower edge and the breastbone. In the effort to maintain body balance over a central support, the medial pull of the musculature causes the limbs to swing inward over the narrowing portion of the chest. The direction of pull is indicated in the diagrams by the dark line (scapula ridge) which appears to shift as the near blade glides over the ribs. As the shoulder moves rearward the action is slightly lateral due to the increase in spring of rib.

Shoulder Movement at the Trot (*continued*)

There is some undulation in the topline as drive from the rear quarters transfers weight from one diagonal pair of legs to the other, when for a split second all four feet are off the ground (fig. 5 and 7). The brief suspension is easier to detect in some breeds than in others, and among individuals within a breed. It depends on springiness of gait, quality of conformation, and soundness, and is referred to as **moving easily** or **moving heavily**.

SHOULDER MOVEMENT AT THE GALLOP

Shoulder excursion at the gallop is far greater than at the trot, with extreme extension of the forelimbs. The lift is emphasized by powerful leverage of the upper arms and strong rearing action in the hindquarters, which thrusts the trunk upward into the flight phases of each stride. Note baselines. Here shown is the double suspension rotary gallop, in which there are two flight phases during each full stride. "Rotary" refers to sequence of footfall.

Shoulder Movement at the Gallop (*continued*)

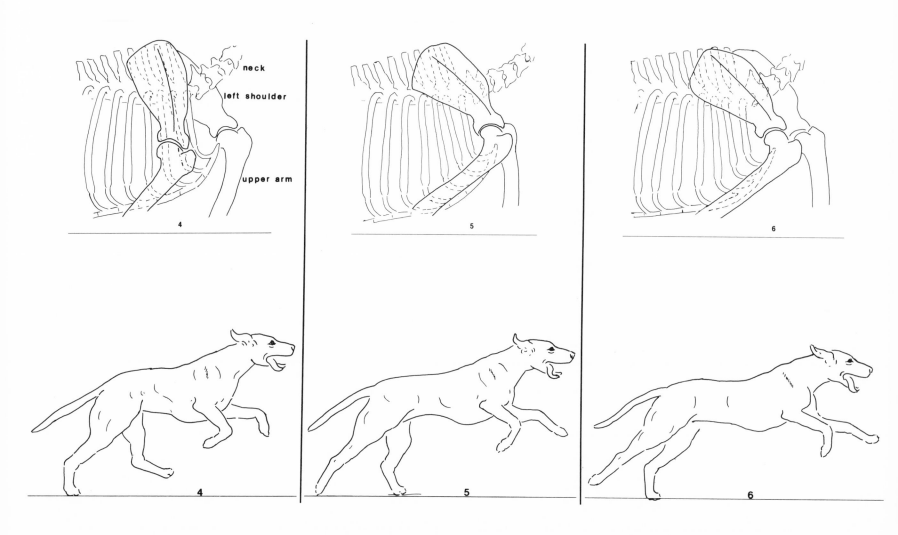

Whether trotting or galloping, correct positioning of the shoulder assembly means that the controlling muscles can serve to optimum advantage, allowing freedom of motion without excessive

Shoulder Movement at the Gallop (*continued*)

slipping at the withers. Add to this qualification a strong working back and hindquarters to balance and we have the essential ingredients for an enduring, ground-covering gait.

Loose Shoulders
—What Happens Inside

The terrier shown here is the subject of the diagrams on Pages 79, 80 and 81.

The diagrams show excessive vertical action in the shoulders. The chest drops low within the front assembly and the upper blades rise abnormally high above the tips of the withers. A "low slung" chest is characteristic of some breeds, but if the conformation is faulty it hampers freedom of action. This terrier's front assembly is not balanced, reach of the forelimbs is restricted, and his paddling gait causes the central body to twist and roll. We might add that poor condition can accentuate the trouble.

The subject of these diagrams also had lateral patella luxation, which is a slipping of the knee cap from its groove at the base of the femur. This unsoundness accentuated his gaiting problem by making the rear limbs swing outward. Patella luxation is more often medial, in which the knee cap slips inward, showing symptoms such as are illustrated on Page 104.

Loose Shoulders—What Happens Inside

left
shoulder

neck

upper arm

6

elbow   forearm

7

8

6

7

8

Another Look at Loose Shoulders

Faulty placement of the shoulders against the chest wall reduces muscular support needed for firm control of the limbs. These illustrations show the blades steeply set and too far forward, causing the neck to appear short. The entire shoulder assembly lacks balance, a fault that in this case causes rocking, crossing, paddling, toeing in and other departures from good movement.

Notice the tips of the blades, which rise and drop in stilted fashion with each step. Loose shoulders do not carry the central body firmly and smoothly.

This dog has a short rib-cage and long coupling, contributing to a weak topline. This is not a working back, as much energy is lost in bouncing up and down and in twisting from side to side. The lack of quality was evident as a young puppy.

The Flexible Shoulder

Well-built hindquarters and flexible shoulders provide stamina for trailing with nose to the ground.

Care must be taken to distinguish faulty "loose" shoulders with too much play at the withers from the muscular flexible shoulders normal for breeds having occupational requirements that permit the body to drop between the shoulders in trailing or crouching. Hounds and spaniels may exhibit such working posture, and anyone who has watched herding dogs creeping alertly behind restless livestock, ready to turn in a flash to control breakaways, can appreciate the need for front-end flexibility as a useful and even life-saving tool.

7.

Heads and Tails . . .

And A Few Other Views

Semantics and Optical Illusion
Can Cause Confusion in
Understanding Gait

A FEW TERMS cause considerable misunderstanding about front and rear action, simply because they are used without clear definition. Expressions such as *parallel, standing straight, moving straight, inclining inward, moving close, toeing in, moving on the same plane, parallel tracks, parallel hocks, single tracking,* and others, not only confuse newcomers, but now and then cause lively discussion among some who have been in the dog game for many years.

The unfortunate aspect of this problem of semantics is that it occasionally permits one to condone certain faulty action, or casts a shadow on action that is correct. It is also a possible reason for faults being perpetuated by innocent parties who try to breed dogs to move in a way never intended by nature. There is a common fallacy, for example, that trotting dogs should move with their legs parallel with each other. Surely such thinking must be influenced by optical illusion, for slow motion photography has long since shown that normal leg movement inclines slightly inward, dependent—of course—on the type of dog and his rate of travel. Misunderstanding of this principle has brought the unjust criticism of "moving too close" on many a dog that actually is moving well. Parallel movement is contrary to nature's laws of balance and motion. Breeders who try to achieve it must sacrifice angulation, and handlers who try to achieve it must resort to tight leads, substituting stilted short action for good natural reach.

The sequence sketches that follow illustrate variations in gaiting as dogs come and go from the viewer, and should help to clarify more of the common faults that often puzzle us.

The Normal Stance
"Parallel" and "Standing Straight"

A dog of good structure stands naturally with his weight evenly distributed at the four corners of his body. Seen from the rear, the legs appear to stand parallel to each other and reasonably straight from hip through stifle and hock to pads.

Viewed from the front, as in the drawing (Fig. B) on P. 92, the column of support from shoulder joint through elbow and carpals to pads is also reasonably straight. The natural tendency of the toes to stand just off the vertical line is for balance, much as a human stands with his feet turned slightly outward, or as a sprinter—just before take-off—rests in forward position, with his fingers on the ground.

In this standing position, the dog's legs are parallel, and may seem to appear parallel as he starts to walk because at the walk the body is supported by three legs with each step and there is little problem with balance. However, as the dog moves faster there is a natural tendency for the limbs to reach inward, called "convergence" or "the tendency to single track." How and why a dog does this is discussed in the following pages.

HIP JOINT

STIFLE

HOCK

REAR PASTERN

Normal Leg Position at the Trot
"Moving Straight"

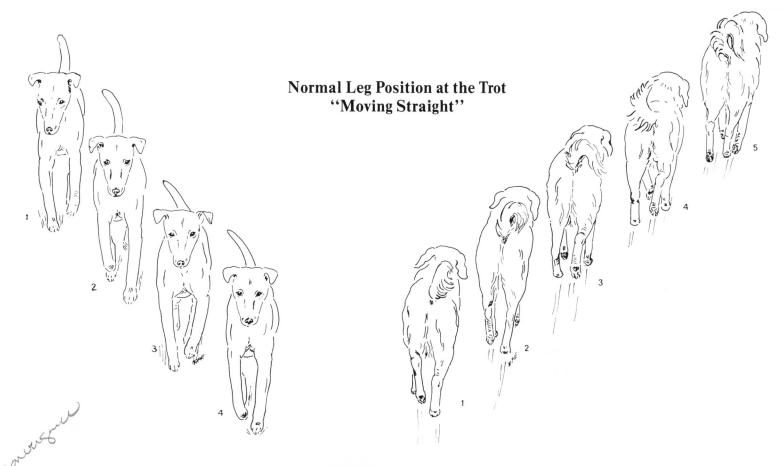

When a dog breaks into a trot, his body is supported by only two legs at a time, which move as alternating diagonal pairs. He must therefore balance himself, as nearly as possible, over a center column of support, in order to travel easily and efficiently; otherwise, he will sway from side to side. To achieve balance, his legs angle inward toward a center line beneath his body, and the greater the speed, the closer they come to tracking on a straight line, much as a human runs with one foot in front of the other to keep his body from rocking. Variations in the dog's height, breadth of body, and length of leg, influence the extent to which the legs incline inward, but all dogs make the effort—regardless of breed or type.

The angle of inclination begins with the shoulders and hips and in the majority of breeds the limbs should remain relatively straight, even as they flex or extend. Such action is described as "moving straight". Flexion in the carpal joint keeps the swing legs from interfering with the supporting legs. The natural law of balance is one of the most important factors in understanding gait as dogs come and go from the viewer. Normal convergence should never be confused with the fault of "moving close."

SINGLE TRACKING. Many dogs single track as they move faster, all footprints falling on a single line of travel.

PARALLEL TRACKING. Others leave parallel tracks, where the footprints fall wider apart on either side of the center line of travel. Speed and build influence the degree to which the limbs incline inward.

The criteria of judgment is not whether a dog single tracks, or whether he has a wider footfall; it is *how* and *why* he moves as he does that must be understood and evaluated against overall conformation and the purpose for which the breed was developed. Regardless of differences, the principle of seeking balanced support remains the same for all, as this is Nature's method of offsetting wasteful action that reduces efficiency.

The Physical Reasons for Limb Convergence Toward A Center Line of Travel

To more clearly understand the principle of convergence—or how a dog tries to maintain body balance over a central support as he moves out of a walk—it is important to visualize how the shoulder blades are positioned against the chest wall. The ribcages of all dogs are oval in shape, but some are rounder than others, some are slimmer, some shallower, some deeper, some shorter and some longer. However, the chest of every dog tapers toward the front end, where there is diminishing spring of rib, and the sternum slopes upward toward the manubrium.

Against this narrowing portion, each shoulder blade rests—as the dog stands—in what might be described as a three-directional position. Thus, when the shoulder assembly goes into action, the forelimbs naturally tend to reach toward the center line of travel.

1. The shoulder blades slant up and back from lower to upper edge. *See Fig. A.*
2. The blades set at an angle that is oblique, not parallel, to the spinal column. *See Fig. B.*
3. The blades lie in toward the withers from shoulder joints to upper tip. *Figs. C and D.*

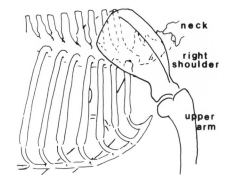

Fig. A. Viewed from the side, *the shoulder blade slants up and back from its lowest edge.* "Shoulder layback" is the expression commonly used in reference to the degree of slope. When the dog moves, the blades swing from the upper rims.

SPINOUS PROCESS
1st bone of withers

T1

SCAPULA SPINE

ACROMION
point of shoulder

MANUBRIUM
breastbone

ACROMION

SHOULDER JOINT

HUMERUS
upper arm

ELBOW

FOREARM

TRAPEZIUS

STERNOMASTOID

DELTOID

BRACHIOCEPHALIC

PECTORAL

TRICEPS

BICEPS

Fig. B. Because of the contour of the forechest, where the ribs are quite flat, *the shoulder blades set at an angle that is oblique—not parallel—to the spine.* The forward edges are deeply imbedded in muscle, thus difficult to feel, and for this reason are often confused with the scapula spines. This oblique position has a direct bearing on limb movement because as the blades glide over the ribs the lift and swing is slightly inward.

Fig. C. Illustrating some of the major muscles that control the forelimbs and help support the trunk as it is carried, sling-like, within the pectoral girdle (front assembly). As previously mentioned, the dog has no collarbone to serve as a stabilizing buttress or strut between the lower blades and the breastbone. This places considerable stress on the muscles and gives rise to thick bones at the shoulder joint and noticeable prominence to the acromion (point of shoulder) which projects outward from the lower end of the scapula spine. The muscles sketched in the above diagram are an important factor in lifting, extending and retracting the forelimbs, as well as in controlling body balance as the dog's speed increases.

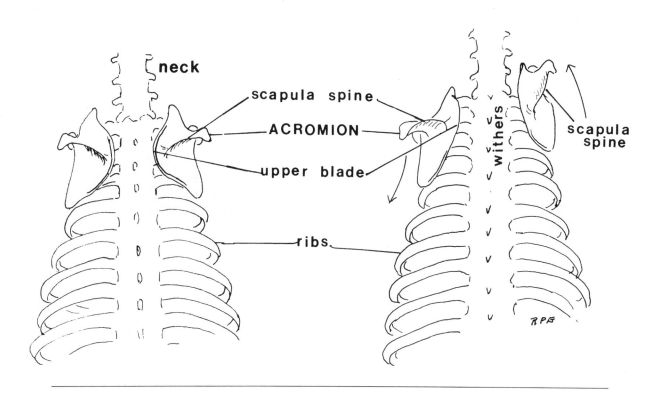

Fig. D. *The shoulders lie in against the withers.* The diagram above illustrates the dorsal aspect of scapulae position, as one looks down on the dog's back. The space between the upper tips often puzzles us as we run our hands down the base of the neck. This spacing is influenced by the type of dog, length and slant of the blades, shape of the ribcage, and the dog's physical condition. In a few breeds the scapula rims tend to rise above the apex of the withers, but most are on a level or just below. It is not always a question of "the closer the better," because it is possible for too narrow a chest combined with steeply set blades to create a pinching effect at the upper tips that hampers free movement. (See Fig. B for front view.)

spacing of withers

93

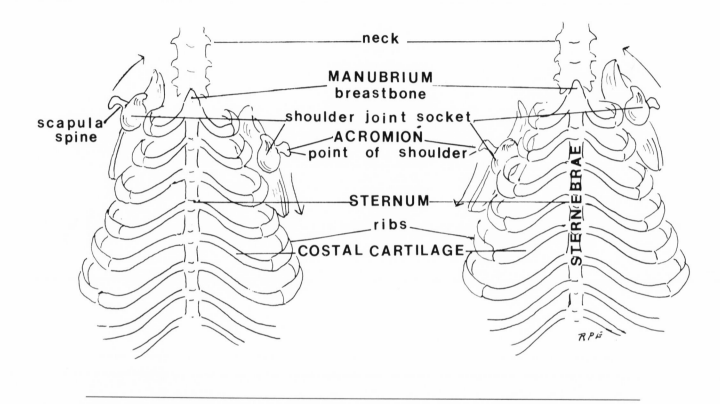

neck

MANUBRIUM
breastbone

shoulder joint socket

ACROMION

point of shoulder

scapula
spine

STERNUM

ribs

COSTAL CARTILAGE

STERNEBRAE

RPE

Fig. E. These diagrams are interpreted from dorsoventral cineradiographic studies showing the ribcage from beneath the dog. While the blades may look like flying saucers (!), the study shows how they glide back and forth along the narrowing contour of the forechest. For the sake of clarity, the upper arms and lower legs are not included—thus only the fossae, or shoulder joint sockets, are visible. From this angle, note how the acromion and the scapula spine jut out prominently from the flatter part of each blade. This is to provide adequate bone for the attachment of heavy muscling needed to stabilize and control movement of the blades, in the absence of the collarbone.

While the joints and muscles are arranged to move the limbs in the direction of travel, the ball and socket design of the hip sockets lends added flexibility to the rear quarters.

Legs "Moving on the Same Plane"

Each leg should move in line with the leg ahead of, or behind it, inclining inward no more and no less. Viewed directly from the rear, the hind legs should tend to cover the plane of the front, and vice versa. There should be no twisting of the joints other than the normal flexibility provided by nature for the passing legs to avoid interference with the legs that are in support. But there are a few exceptions—see next page.

A few breeds, such as the Bulldog or Pekingese, are normally broader in the front quarters than they are in the rear. This type of conformation causes the hind feet to track within the footfall of the front. The wide diagonal thrust contributes to a characteristic, almost swaggering or rolling action, but this should not be exaggerated.

Legs "Not Moving on the Same Plane" (*fault*)

When the hind feet do not follow the tracks made by the front feet, the legs are not inclining inward to the same extent and the action is faulty. Many gaiting faults fall under this category. But again, there are exceptions—see the facing page.

Front feet moving wide, hind feet moving on center line.

Hind feet moving wide, front feet moving on center line.

MOVING WIDE IN FRONT and tracking on a single line in the rear. In this illustration, the left hock tends to twist as it bears weight.

TRACKING TOO WIDE BEHIND. This type of action may be caused by tight ligaments, or may indicate trouble in the stifle joints.

"Crabbing" (*fault*)

"Crabbing" is a common fault, in which the dog moves with his body at an angle to the line of travel. The action is frequently due to more angulation in the rear than in the front, in combination with a short, stiff back.

When a dog takes longer steps with his hind legs than with his forelimbs, he can avoid striking or interfering by trotting with his hindquarters swung to one side. However, because the legs do not "move on the same plane," the gait is awkward and inefficient.

Crabbing may also indicate spinal injury, as the dog twists to relieve strain. Occasionally, it is the result of habit from constant heeling and watching the owner.

The term "crabbing" originates with the seacrab, which crawls forward in sidewise fashion. The fault is also occasionally referred to as "yawing," or as "side-winding." Careless handling or lack of leash training often causes dogs that normally would move straight to "crab."

"Crabbing" and
"Crossing in the Rear"
(*faults*)

1

2

3

4

Below: **Roached Back with "Crabbing"** (*faults*)

A roached back is a stiff back, often seen with crabbing or pacing. This particular dog is taller than he is long, giving him proportions that accentuate the problem of trying to avoid leg interference. A roached back is often the result of strain or spinal disorder.

1

2

3

4

1

2

3

4

5

1

2

3

4

5

"Weaving" or "Knitting and Purling"
(*fault*)

Well nicknamed is this unsound action,
which starts with twisting elbows, and
ends with crisscrossing pasterns and
toeing out.

"Moving Close" and "Stifles Out" (*faults*)

When the hocks turn in, and the pasterns drop straight to the ground and move parallel to one another, the dog is "moving close" in the rear. In some cases, as in this illustration, the stifle is also thrown out of line. Action of this sort places severe strain on ligaments and muscles.

"Moving Close" and "Brushing" (*faults*)

Top: Parallel pasterns are sometimes so close that the legs "brush" in passing.

Below: Interfering and Crossing (*faults*).

102

"Cowhocks" (*fault*)

Cows often stand with their hocks turned in, and their stifles turned out, to accommodate large udders more comfortably. "Cowhocks" in dogs seriously weaken rear thrust.

This dog is not only cowhocked, but is also crossing his legs in front—a fault no doubt accentuated, because he is pulling to one side from his handler.

"Snatching Hocks" (*fault*) — **A symptom of stifle trouble.**

This fault is indicated by a quick outward snatching of the hocks, or sometimes a skipping action, as it passes the supporting leg and twists the rear pastern in beneath the body. It is a compensation for discomfort in the stifle joint and causes noticeable rocking in the rear quarters. The subject of this series illustrates a known case of bilateral (both sides) patella luxation.

"Spread Hocks" (*fault*)

Hocks that turn out are called "spread hocks", "barrel hocks", "divergent hocks", or "hocking out". Like other faults, it shows up in varying degrees of severity. It always causes the feet to "toe in" (just the opposite from "cowhocks", which causes "toeing out").

"Spread hocks", combined with "crossing in front".

Twisting hocks

Out at stifle

1

2

3

4

5

6

"Twisting Hocks" (*fault*)

Also called "rubber hocks" or "weak hocks", this fault differs from "spread hocks" and "cowhocks" in that the joints twist both ways as they flex or bear weight.

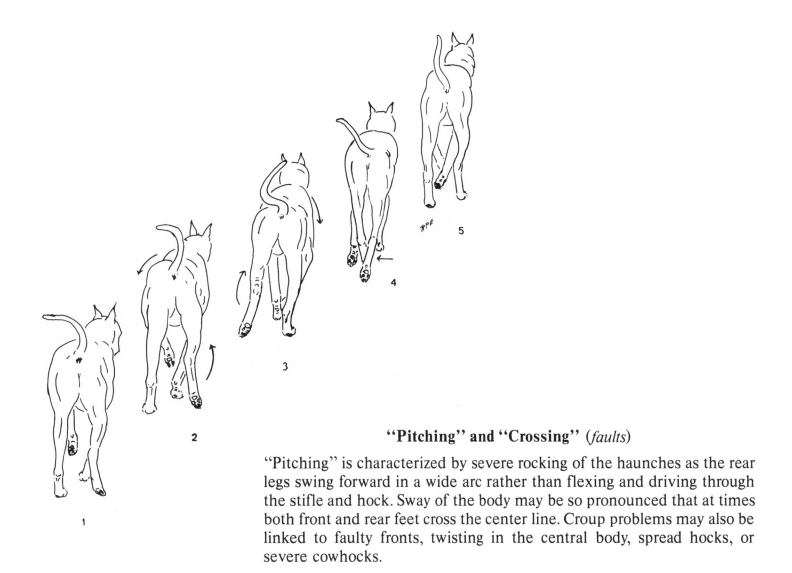

1

2

3

4

5

"Pitching" and "Crossing" (*faults*)

"Pitching" is characterized by severe rocking of the haunches as the rear legs swing forward in a wide arc rather than flexing and driving through the stifle and hock. Sway of the body may be so pronounced that at times both front and rear feet cross the center line. Croup problems may also be linked to faulty fronts, twisting in the central body, spread hocks, or severe cowhocks.

Twisting joints mean wear and tear on ligaments and muscles—more than sufficient reason for complete exhaustion after a day in the field.

"Pitching" combined with "Cowhocks" (*faults*)

109

Because of their structure, short-legged, broadly-built dogs move with some body roll, but those that move well minimize this tendency through the natural inclination of the legs toward a center line of balance beneath their bodies.

Left: Moving well in front, but "toeing out" in the rear ("cowhocks").

Right: Good rear movement.

"Moving too wide" in front,
"Too close" in rear, and
"Toeing in" (*faults*)

"Toeing Out" or the
"East-West Front"
(*fault*)

Arrows point to weak carpal
joints, which bend inward
causing the feet to turn out.

111

Championship Titles Do Not Guarantee Perfection

If you plan to raise dogs, study the pedigrees carefully. Most faults tend to be inherited, and serious defects which become deeply entrenched can imperil the soundness of breeding strains.

5 Toeing in

4

Twisting elbows

Twisting pasterns

Twisting hocks

3

2

Interfering

1

Out at the Elbows (*fault*)

Elbows often cause trouble by "moving out".

113

1

2

3

4

5

RPE

"Tied at the Elbows" or "Paddling"
(*fault*)

is just the opposite sort of action from elbows moving out, and is generally considered a more serious defect because it so severely restricts front movement. Pinching in at the elbows, as well as at the shoulder joints, causes the front legs to swing forward on a stiff outward arc. Because of the wide footfall, the dog is said to travel "basewide", and the body rocks from side to side.

The term "paddling" derives from the swing and dip of the paddle as the canoeist keeps his canoe on course.

Why Dogs Pace

Pacing as a Result of "Square" Body Structure

Mature dogs that are "squarely" built, but tend to stand a bit lower at the withers than at the croup, often develop a natural tendency to avoid leg interference by pacing, rather than trotting. In the lateral action, the body tends to roll as the dog shifts his weight from side to side.

The dog in these illustrations is a natural pacer. In the top sequence, he is pacing easily. In the sequence below, he is trotting awkwardly because he is forced to "crab" to avoid leg interference. Pacing is frowned upon in the show ring, regardless of breed.

Pacing to Avoid Interference (*fault*)

Generally speaking, dogs need a little more length of body than height at the withers, in order to be able to coordinate drive from the rear with reach in the front. A dog that is *too* short usually lacks angulation in one end or the other and often in both. Sometimes, if rear angulation is better he may become a habitual pacer to keep the hind feet from stepping on the front, as illustrated above.

Illustrated below is the same dog trotting awkwardly as the rear legs have to by-pass the front. This is an extreme example of poor foot timing.

Overreaching

Pacing Due to Injury or Roached Back
(fault)

Sometimes pacing is the result of injury or strain in the loin area, or it can be due to too much arch in the back, which restricts action of the croup muscles. A dog will move in the way which is easiest for him, whether it be to alleviate pain, or because of habit resulting from poor conformation.

Pacing and Ambling as "Fatigue" Gaits

This sketch was drawn from a photograph of exhausted sled dogs as they neared the finish line of a race, most of them pacing or ambling to rest muscles weary from trotting and cantering. Here the pace and amble are rightly referred to as "fatigue" gaits, because the dogs have switched to lateral movement to relieve strain.

A Few Hints on Handling

If we plan to exhibit in dogs shows, we should give our dogs the advantage they deserve through careful handling. Good handling brings out the best in a dog. Poor handling can impair his overall appearance, and give the impression of faults that are not really there.

119

Mirrors are a great help in checking your handling.

When the judge requests that you "gait your dog" in the show ring, the straight-on approach is important—but remember, it is the dog, not you, who is under judgment.

A Tight Lead Is Often Detrimental

Swinging from the end of a tight lead causes this dog to "cross" in front.

Side pull on the lead accentuates the dog's tendency to "cross."

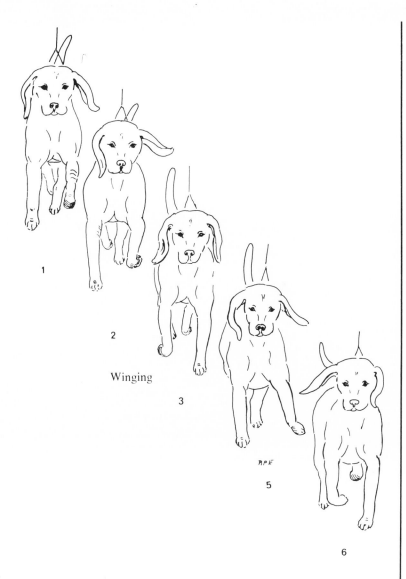

1

2

Winging

3

5

6

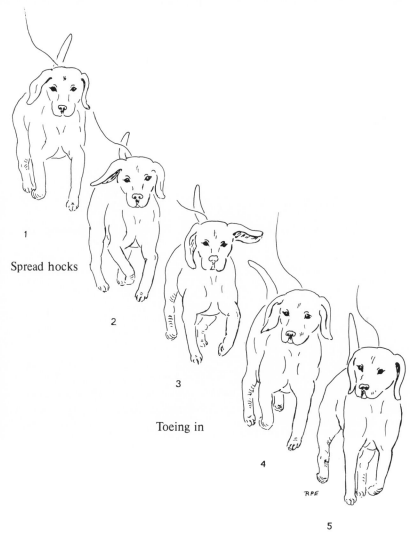

1

Spread hocks

2

3

Toeing in

4

5

"Winging" is usually a natural fault where one or both front feet twist outward as the limbs swing forward, but here the fault is introduced artificially by too tight a lead.

At the judge's request, "Loose lead, please," the same dog trots freely and exhibits his natural inclination to **"move wide in the hocks," "out at the elbows,"** and **"toe in,"** all of which are gaiting flaws.

123

Conclusion

At risk of being considered a "fault finder", the author may appear to have dwelt rather heavily on what makes a dog move incorrectly — and not have stressed enough the features that make him move well. Unfortunately, faults tend to linger in one's impression, and too often override the total perspective. Such an imbalance was not our intent, but if our emphasis has stirred awareness of a few structural pitfalls that threaten the quality of many present day breeds, then it will have served a useful purpose.

Although you might find it difficult to put into words what you are looking for in good movement, you may have sensed it without knowing why. It may be just the feeling of pleasure over the flashy gait of a stylish entry in the show ring, or the thrill of excitement that comes with watching a hunting dog work smoothly across a field and suddenly freeze on point. You may instinctively have sensed the importance of stamina if you have hunted over a retriever that swims strongly and eagerly at the close of a strenuous day in the marshes. Or, if you are one who has handled a willing dog through obedience competition where advanced training demands constant effort in jumping, you have experienced the need for soundness.

Too often puppies are selected solely on the basis of their expression, personality, color, coat texture, or size-traits, which to be sure, give each its special appeal and add to the joy of the owner. But these traits alone are not enough. Structure must also be considered if a breed or a strain is to be kept strong. So it is to the breeders who know what to look for and what to avoid, who know what makes a good dog move well and why, that novices should turn for guidance and learning. Experience is a good teacher, but knowledge—with a little luck!—steers the shortest way to lasting success.

References
— and books of interest

Bracket, Lloyd C. and Horswell, Laurence A., *The Dog In Motion.* Dog World Magazine (USA). August 1961—October 1965.

Brown, Curtis and Thelma, *Art and Science of Judging Dogs,* B & E Publications, Inc., Hollywood, CA.

The Canine, A Veterinary Aid in Anatomical Transparencies, Fromm Laboratories, Inc., Grafton, Wisconsin, 1967.

Ellenberger, Baum, and Dittrich, *An Atlas of Animal Anatomy for Artists,* Dover Publications, Inc., New York, 1967.

Gardiner, Catherine, *Dogs—As a Hobby or Profession,* Vol. I, II. Canine Consultants, Ltd., Ontario, Canada.

Hollenbeck, Leon, *The Dynamics of Canine Gait,* Hollenbeck, Akron, N.Y., 1971.

Horner, Tom, *Take Them Around Please,* Douglas David & Charles, Ltd., Canada, 1975.

Jenkins, Farish A., Jr., *The Movement of the Shoulder in Claviculate and Aclaviculate Mammals,* Department of Biology, Museum of Comparative Zoology, Harvard University, Cambridge, Mass.

————, *Hip Structure and Locomotion in Ambulatory and Cursorial Carnivores,* Department of Biology, Museum of Comparative Zoology, Harvard University, Cambridge, Mass.

Lyon, McDowell, *The Dog In Action,* Howell Book House Inc., N.Y., 1950.

Miller, Christensen and Evans, *Anatomy of the Dog,* W.B. Saunders, Philadelphia, London, 1964.

Miller, Constance, *Search for Truth in Gazehounds,* Gazehound magazine (USA), series in 22 parts— May 1976 through August 1980.

Smythe, R.H., *The Anatomy of Dog Breeding,* Popular Dogs Publishing Co., London, 1962.

————, *Dog Structure and Movement,* Popular Dogs Publishing Co., London, 1970.

————, *The Conformation of the Dog,* Popular Dogs Publishing Co., London, 1957.

Stillman, J.D.B., *The Horse in Motion,* James R. Osgood & Co., Boston, 1882.

"Stonehenge", *The Dogs of the British Islands,* 2nd edition, London, 1872.

BIBLIOGRAPHY

ALL OWNERS of pure-bred dogs will benefit themselves and their dogs by enriching their knowledge of breeds and of canine care, training, breeding, psychology and other important aspects of dog management. The following list of books covers further reading recommended by judges, veterinarians, breeders, trainers and other authorities. Books may be obtained at the finer book stores and pet shops, or through Howell Book House Inc., publishers, New York.

Breed Books

AFGHAN HOUND, Complete	Miller & Gilbert
AIREDALE, New Complete	Edwards
AKITA, Complete	Linderman & Funk
ALASKAN MALAMUTE, Complete	Riddle & Seeley
BASSET HOUND, Complete	Braun
BEAGLE, New Complete	Noted Authorities
BLOODHOUND, Complete	Brey & Reed
BORZOI, Complete	Groshans
BOXER, Complete	Denlinger
BRITTANY SPANIEL, Complete	Riddle
BULLDOG, New Complete	Hanes
BULL TERRIER, New Complete	Eberhard
CAIRN TERRIER, Complete	Marvin
CHESAPEAKE BAY RETRIEVER, Complete	Cherry
CHIHUAHUA, Complete	Noted Authorities
COCKER SPANIEL, New	Kraeuchi
COLLIE, New	Official Publication of the Collie Club of America
DACHSHUND, The New	Meistrell
DALMATIAN, The	Treen
DOBERMAN PINSCHER, New	Walker
ENGLISH SETTER, New Complete	Tuck, Howell & Graef
ENGLISH SPRINGER SPANIEL, New	Goodall & Gasow
FOX TERRIER, New Complete	Silvernail
GERMAN SHEPHERD DOG, New Complete	Bennett
GERMAN SHORTHAIRED POINTER, New	Maxwell
GOLDEN RETRIEVER, Complete	Fischer
GREAT DANE, New Complete	Noted Authorities
GREAT DANE, The—Dogdom's Apollo	Draper
GREAT PYRENEES, Complete	Strang & Giffin
IRISH SETTER, New	Thompson
IRISH WOLFHOUND, Complete	Starbuck
KEESHOND, Complete	Peterson
LABRADOR RETRIEVER, Complete	Warwick
LHASA APSO, Complete	Herbel
MINIATURE SCHNAUZER, Complete	Eskrigge
NEWFOUNDLAND, New Complete	Chern
NORWEGIAN ELKHOUND, New Complete	Wallo
OLD ENGLISH SHEEPDOG, Complete	Mandeville
PEKINGESE, Quigley Book of	Quigley
PEMBROKE WELSH CORGI, Complete	Sargent & Harper
POODLE, New Complete	Hopkins & Irick
POODLE CLIPPING AND GROOMING BOOK, Complete	Kalstone
PULI, Complete	Owen
SAMOYED, Complete	Ward
SCHIPPERKE, Official Book of	Root, Martin, Kent
SCOTTISH TERRIER, New Complete	Marvin
SHETLAND SHEEPDOG, The New	Riddle
SHIH TZU, Joy of Owning	Seranne
SHIH TZU, The (English)	Dadds
SIBERIAN HUSKY, Complete	Demidoff
TERRIERS, The Book of All	Marvin
WEST HIGHLAND WHITE TERRIER, Complete	Marvin
WHIPPET, Complete	Pegram
YORKSHIRE TERRIER, Complete	Gordon & Bennett

Breeding

ART OF BREEDING BETTER DOGS, New	Onstott
BREEDING YOUR OWN SHOW DOG	Seranne
HOW TO BREED DOGS	Whitney
HOW PUPPIES ARE BORN	Prine
INHERITANCE OF COAT COLOR IN DOGS	Little

Care and Training

DOG OBEDIENCE, Complete Book of	Saunders
NOVICE, OPEN AND UTILITY COURSES	Saunders
DOG CARE AND TRAINING FOR BOYS AND GIRLS	Saunders
DOG NUTRITION, Collins Guide to	Collins
DOG TRAINING FOR KIDS	Benjamin
DOG TRAINING, Koehler Method of	Koehler
DOG TRAINING, Step by Step Manual	Volhard & Fisher
GO FIND! Training Your Dog to Track	Davis
GUARD DOG TRAINING, Koehler Method of	Koehler
OPEN OBEDIENCE FOR RING, HOME AND FIELD, Koehler Method of	Koehler
STONE GUIDE TO DOG GROOMING FOR ALL BREEDS	Stone
SUCCESSFUL DOG TRAINING, The Pearsall Guide to	Pearsall
TOY DOGS, Kalstone Guide to Grooming All	Kalstone
TRAINING THE RETRIEVER	Kersley
TRAINING YOUR DOG TO WIN OBEDIENCE TITLES	Morsell
TRAIN YOUR OWN GUN DOG, How to	Goodall
UTILITY DOG TRAINING, Koehler Method of	Koehler
VETERINARY HANDBOOK, Dog Owner's Home	Carlson & Giffin

General

CANINE TERMINOLOGY	Spira
COMPLETE DOG BOOK, The	Official Publication of American Kennel Club
DOG IN ACTION, The	Lyon
DOG BEHAVIOR, New Knowledge of	Pfaffenberger
DOG JUDGE'S HANDBOOK	Tietjen
DOG JUDGING, Nicholas Guide to	Nicholas
DOG PEOPLE ARE CRAZY	Riddle
DOG PSYCHOLOGY	Whitney
DOGSTEPS, Illustrated Gait at a Glance	Elliott
DOG TRICKS	Haggerty & Benjamin
ENCYCLOPEDIA OF DOGS, International	Dangerfield, Howell & Riddle
FROM RICHES TO BITCHES	Shattuck
IN STITCHES OVER BITCHES	Shattuck
JUNIOR SHOWMANSHIP HANDBOOK	Brown & Mason
MY TIMES WITH DOGS	Fletcher
OUR PUPPY'S BABY BOOK (blue or pink)	
SUCCESSFUL DOG SHOWING, Forsyth Guide to	Forsyth
TRIM, GROOM AND SHOW YOUR DOG, How to	Saunders
WHY DOES YOUR DOG DO THAT?	Bergman
WILD DOGS in Life and Legend	Riddle
WORLD OF SLED DOGS, From Siberia to Sport Racing	Coppinger